life begins for puppies

life begins Lilo Hess
for puppies

Charles Scribner's Sons • New York

Printed in the United States of America/1 3 5 7 9 11 13 15 17 19 MD/C 20 18 16 14 12 10 8 6 4 2
Library of Congress Catalog Card Number 77-28256/ISBN 0-684-15652-0

I have a dog named Poco. She is a Shetland Sheepdog bitch (female dog) about two years old, and very loving and affectionate. Shetland Sheepdogs look like miniature Collies, but they are a separate breed. They originated in the Shetland Islands off Scotland where they were used to herd the small cattle for which the islands are well known. Today they are mostly kept as pets and loyal companions, but their ability to work and to please their masters remains deeply implanted in the breed. Because of those characteristics the Shetland Sheepdog—or Sheltie, as it is usually called—excels in obedience competitions and sheepherding trials.

I saw Poco for the first time in an animal shelter near my home. I had gone there to donate some food for the many homeless and abandoned dogs and cats that find temporary shelter there. It was a warm day in May, and most of the dogs were in outdoor cages. The runs on one side of the building housed the puppies. They were of all ages, all colors, and all shapes and sizes, but they had one thing in common—they were all homeless and unloved. On the other side of the building identical cages housed the fully grown dogs, and here, too, was the same variety. Some were old and sickly, some young and bouncy. Most of them were thin, nervous, and bewildered. In one of the cages I saw a Sheltie. She was jumpy and her dirty fur was matted and thin. I was told that she had been found running along the highway and was taken to the shelter by a motorist who had spent considerable time coaxing the shy animal to come to him. She wore no license or identification and no one had claimed her. Now she was up for adoption. I already had one Sheltie, two German Shepherds, and four cats at home and did not want another dog, but when she looked at me with her dark almond-shaped eyes in her sensitive face, I could not resist. I adopted her.

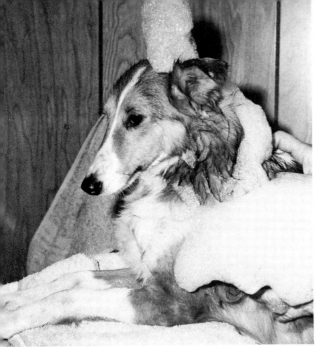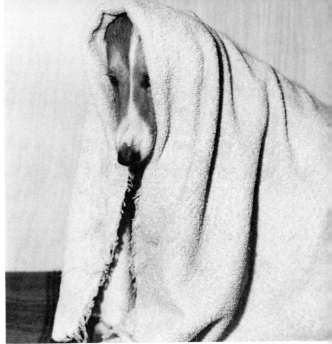

She came with me very willingly, and when we reached home she seemed eager to go into the house. Unfortunately she did not get a warm welcome from the other Sheltie, but there was no fight and after a little snarling they just kept out of each other's way. The two German Shepherds ignored her. I named the new dog Poco.

After Poco had rested a while and inspected her new home, I gave her a bath with a good flea-killing shampoo. She shivered and looked unhappy with all that soap foam over her, but after she was wrapped in towels and dried thoroughly, she looked and seemed to feel much better and wagged her tail for the first time. Then she jumped onto the bed and settled down for a nap as if she had always been used to such luxury.

After a few days Poco was an accepted member of the family, and all the cats and dogs had made their peace with her. She followed me about the house or sat at my feet, and when I went out she lay by the door and quietly awaited my return. She had a tremendous appetite and ate more than I had thought possible for such a small animal.

After she had been with me for almost four weeks I noticed how much weight she had put on in this short time. When she sat on the floor with her back turned to me, she looked almost double the size she had been. She also had lost her bounce and vitality, and she had a quiet, matronly look about her. I looked at her more closely and saw that her breast was a little fuller and her nipples were larger.

I diagnosed this as a case of false pregnancy, a condition that occurs often in bitches. The dog goes through all the symptoms of pregnancy, even producing milk, without really being pregnant. But four days later I knew that this pregnancy was real. When Poco was resting on her side, I noticed the gentle turns and kicks of puppies inside her.

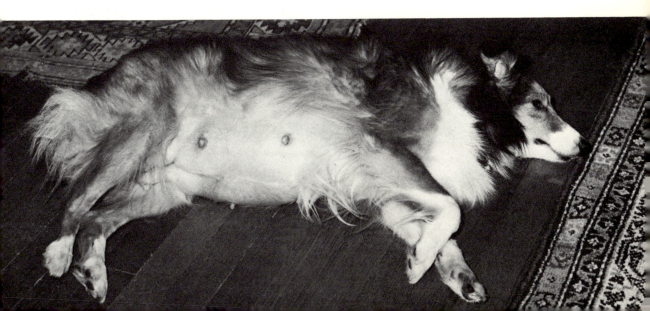

I was very distressed. It is never advisable to raise puppies that are not planned for or wanted. Who was the sire (or father) of these pups? What kind of strange mixture would they turn out to be? Would I be able to find good, steady homes for them?

But those worries had to be put aside for the time being in order to get ready for the whelping, as the process of giving

birth in dogs is called. (Newborn puppies are often referred to as whelps.) No matter how often a person has witnessed the miracle of birth, it never loses its fascination, and in spite of the circumstances, I started to look forward to the event.

At last it seemed that Poco's time was very close at hand. The gestation period (or pregnancy) in dogs is usually sixty-three days, but, as in all mammals, including humans, the birth can occur a little sooner or later.

A box had to be found in which the puppies could be born and live for the first few weeks. It could be a roomy cardboard box, or a more sturdy one made out of plywood or a similar material. The box needed a removable front so that the bitch could get in and out without having to jump over the front during her pregnant period. Later the front could be replaced to keep the puppies from falling or walking out. I had a plywood box built, lined it with newspaper, and put it in a small spare room so that Poco and her babies could have privacy. Any quiet out-of-the-way place in the house is suitable for use as a nursery.

When Poco was introduced to the box, she seemed to know right away that it was meant for her use. She immediately stretched out in it—but only for a few moments; then she got up and pulled out all the neatly folded newspaper and tore it. She was very restless. I thought she might prefer to have shredded newspaper so she could make a sort of nest with it, as I had been told many dogs do; but that, too, was pushed out of the box. That day and the next Poco stayed near her box or stayed inside for short periods. She panted a great deal and looked very uncomfortable.

It is often hard to tell exactly when a bitch is ready to whelp. One test many dog breeders make is to take the animal's temperature twice a day. If it is 100 degrees F. (about 38 degrees C.) or below and does not rise by the next reading, the puppies should arrive within twenty-four hours. The normal temperature of dogs is about 102 degrees F. (about 39 degrees C.).

Most dogs know exactly what to do when their young are born. They do this by instinct. (Instincts are habits and skills an animal is born with and knows without having to learn or experience them.) But some of our domestic animals, especially dogs, have been pampered and bred so that they have lost many of their natural instincts. Some dogs do not know what to do and do not seem to care what happens to their babies. Human help is needed if the pups are to be saved. Other dogs are excellent mothers from the start. I intended to stay with Poco just in case she needed me, and also to photograph the birth if possible.

It was almost midnight when Poco had the first contractions. She alternately paced the floor and lay down in her box. Then suddenly, while she was in the box, the water bag broke and the first puppy slid out immediately after that.

Like all newborn puppies, it was encased in a membrane

sac and attached by a tube, called the umbilical cord, to the placenta (afterbirth). The placenta is an organ that provides the unborn baby with nourishment and oxygen through the umbilical cord. At birth all this is expelled. The thin membrane that surrounds the baby must be broken quickly so that the puppy can start to breathe on its own. The mother severs

the umbilical cord by chewing it off about 2 or 3 inches (5 to 7½ centimeters) from the baby's body. Then she often, but not always, eats the afterbirth, which is full of nutrients.

If the bitch does not immediately break the sac over the baby's face and lick its nose and mouth to clear away any mucus, the pup will smother. An inexperienced bitch sometimes does not do it right or quickly, so most breeders stay close by when their dogs whelp. Often the sac breaks by itself as the baby comes down the birth canal and emerges, but the newborn still needs to be cleaned.

Poco did everything very efficiently and swiftly. She cleaned the baby all over and rolled it about, which helped to stimulate its circulation and breathing. After Poco had finished, I picked

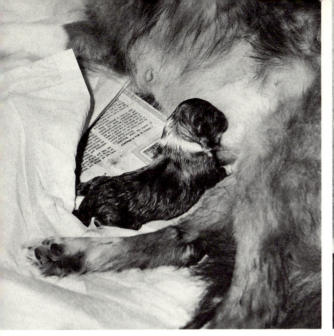

the baby up to record its sex, weight, and color markings. It was a male weighing about 8 ounces, and it was mostly brown with just a narrow white band around its neck, a white tip on the tail, and some white on its legs. While I was looking at the baby, Poco cleaned herself up and ate the afterbirth. When I returned the baby to her, she pushed it immediately toward one of her nipples, and the puppy suckled vigorously.

The first milklike substance that the mother dog produces is called colostrum and contains many antibodies, nutrients, and vitamins that are very important for a new puppy. It helps to immunize the baby against the germs and bacteria that surround it in its new environment. About twenty-four hours after birth the colostrum changes to milk and flows more freely.

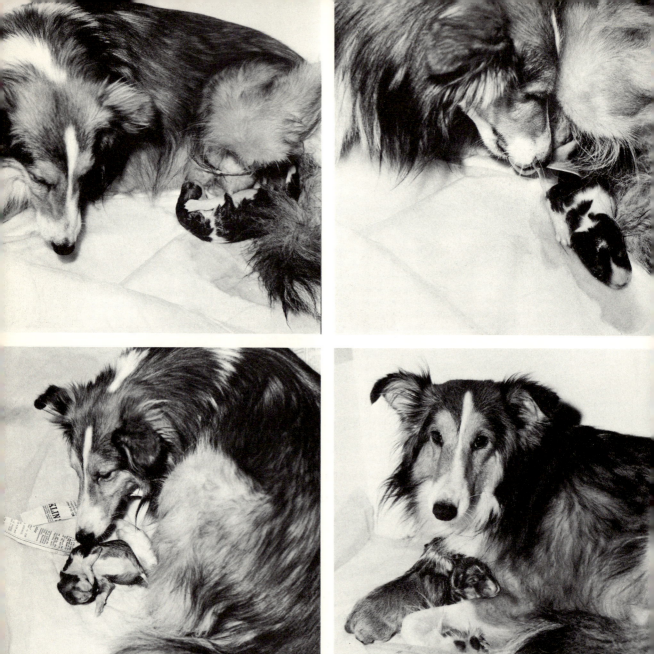

The second pup arrived almost one and a half hours later, and Poco had to strain and push to expel it. The sac was broken when the puppy emerged, and Poco cleaned its nostrils and face and after that chewed off the umbilical cord. This puppy was large, and its fur looked black, with white markings. It was a female and weighed 8½ ounces. Poco looked very tired, so while her two puppies nursed, I gave her a little ice cream, which is refreshing and nourishing. She licked the dish clean and then licked my hand. An hour later, when Poco and the puppies were dozing, a sharp contraction startled Poco awake. She pushed the puppies aside and a small female, weighing in at 7.7 ounces, arrived. She was mostly brown with a half circle of white on her neck.

Two hours went by, and I was not sure if any more puppies would arrive. Then Poco heaved a deep sigh and raised up a little, and a fourth puppy emerged. Usually when a puppy is born in a sac it lays fairly still until its mother has cleaned away the membrane and mucus and it is breathing. This little pup wiggled and struggled as soon as it emerged and tore the membrane itself. It was a male and weighed almost 8 ounces. It had a very reddish color with a pretty white ruff around its neck and a small white mark on its forehead. I called the puppy Amber, the only one that had a name at this early age.

From the relaxed expression on Poco's face I could see that no more puppies were to be expected. I gave Poco some warm milk and took her outside to relieve herself. Then I changed the bedding in the box so that everyone was warm and dry. Poco looked pleased and her tail was wagging; she curled up next to her tiny brood and they all slept for many hours. The birth of Poco's four puppies had taken almost seven hours.

Every bitch gives birth in a similar way. Some have their babies at short intervals; others, like Poco, have a long wait between the births. Some dogs lay on their side, some squat, some even stand when the whelp emerges. Some bitches eat the afterbirth, others do not. Some need human help when whelping, especially the small, delicate breeds or those with very large heads. Some breeds cannot chew off the umbilical cord because of the structure of their teeth and jaws. Some dogs reject their offspring for one reason or another, while others are protective and devoted mothers. Some dogs have such large litters that they cannot nurse all the puppies, and if the babies are to survive some of them have to be bottle-fed.

Only the female dog takes care of the litter. Among *wild* relatives of the dog, such as wolves or foxes, the father has an important part in raising the young. He helps to provide food and guard the family.

About twelve hours after their birth, the puppies looked very different. Their short, baby fur looked much fluffier. They had filled out a little as if they had already gained weight, and their color looked much lighter. I was surprised to see that the little female that had been almost black with white markings was now a rich sable color with white. All the puppies looked like true Sheltie puppies to me.

Shetland Sheepdogs, like Collies, have long, slender muzzles as adults, but the pups have blunt, oval faces. It takes several months of growth until the muzzle is as long, proportionately, as that of the adult.

Small puppies of many breeds often look very different from their parents.

The long, slender muzzle and head of the aristocratic-looking Afghan Hound is not present in the very young pups. Like the Shelties, they have egg-shaped heads and blunt muzzles. It takes about six months for them to look like their parents. A litter of Afghan pups can also have many different colors and shades, even if both parents have the same coloring.

The silver-gray Poodle has pitch-black babies, and it takes four to five months for the silver color to show. The beautiful little Yorkshire Terrier is steel blue and red-gold as an adult, but the puppies are all-black at birth. The adult color grows in slowly, and only at the age of six to nine months do the dogs

AFGHAN HOUND

YORKSHIRE TERRIER

resemble their breed in coloration. The Dalmatian is well known for its spotted coat, but the babies are born all-white. Faint spots start to appear after ten days and get darker and larger as the pups grow older.

There are also many breeds of dogs in which the puppies resemble their parents almost from the start; the Norwegian Elkhound is one example.

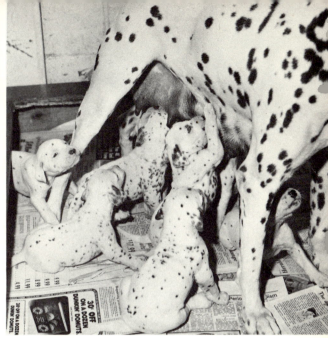

DALMATIAN

NORWEGIAN ELKHOUND

The first few days of the life of Poco's puppies passed very quietly. The babies suckled and slept most of the day, and they chirped like little birds in the nest when their mother got up or if they could not find the nipple right away. Poco spent very little time away from them. She slept a lot, too, with her children pressed close against her. She cleaned them over and over and, by licking, stimulated them to relieve themselves. Very young animals, wild and domestic, need their mother to help them urinate and defecate until they are two or four weeks old. Most dog mothers clean up after their babies as long as they are nursing, but once the pups eat other food, the mother stops.

On the second day the small piece of umbilical cord that the mother had left on each baby started to dry up, and on the third day it fell off.

When their mother was not with them, the pups huddled together to keep warm, and probably for comfort and companionship as well. They were too weak to walk, but they could push themselves about with a swimming motion.

Poco left her pups now for longer and longer periods and often lay down outside the box, ready to comfort or feed her babies when needed. From the fourth day on she also left the nursery for a little while to visit with her human friends. When she returned to the box, she usually lay down on the opposite side from where her puppies were sleeping. It almost seemed as if she did it deliberately so that the pups had to exercise as they crawled and wiggled toward her. Although they were still blind and could not hear, they quickly found her and were rewarded with licks and a fresh supply of milk. The puppies drank so much that it took several hours to replenish the milk. Poco, too, had an enormous appetite—she ate three times her regular amount. I supplemented her food with vitamins, calcium, egg yolk, chicken broth, and fresh milk.

On the eighth day the pups made shaky and not very successful attempts to walk. They could hold up their heads, and they looked and acted more like little dogs are supposed to look and act.

On the tenth day their eyes opened, but they could not see very much. They still bumped into things and each other, just as they had done before. A few days later their vision seemed to have improved considerably. All dogs are color-blind and see the world only in varying shades of gray.

The puppies had gained weight steadily and now were twice their birth weight.

The pups could not hear until the fourteenth day. As soon as their ears were open, they responded to sounds around them, but it seemed that they could not quite locate the direction from which the sound came. If I called and clapped my hands, all four pups heard it, but they looked in all different directions. If I called and tapped the floor, the vibration made them all look directly at me.

At this time they also started to stand up on shaky legs and were able to take a few steps before they collapsed into a heap again.

The babies were more independent now and often slept by themselves, but as soon as they awoke they sought each other's company again. The days and nights still passed very quietly and peacefully. Eating, sleeping, and a little wiggling and stumbling about were their main activities.

A sudden noticeable change came when they were three weeks old. The puppies stayed awake for longer periods, and they had learned to walk and started to play. At first they played very slowly, cautiously, and gently, lifting up one paw to touch a neighbor's back or head, circling each other, pulling an ear just a bit, or catching another puppy's wagging tail. Every day their play became livelier and rougher, and lasted longer. They had mock fights, but they howled loudly if one puppy nipped another one too hard. They emitted funny little threatening barks and made a gurgling sound that probably was supposed to be a growl.

Up to now Poco had been her babies' sole source of food. But now, after four weeks, her milk supply was not enough anymore, so I provided extra food for the babies twice a day. One at a time I taught the puppies how to lap food from a dish, and it took them only minutes to get the idea. They were very eager to get the extra food. The formula I gave them consisted of one part evaporated milk and one part water. I mixed in a little pablum or oatmeal to give the liquid a bit more substance. After a few days, I added lean, finely ground beef. The puppies weighed 4 pounds each at the age of four weeks.

The old whelping box was getting very crowded with four growing, tumbling, and roughhousing puppies in it. Poco had no room to stretch out on the few occasions she wanted to nurse the family, so she did it standing up. The puppies also became more curious about the world outside the box and kept looking out longingly. Then one day, one puppy jumped out and the others soon followed. From that day on there was no confining them in the box.

Since the weather was warm and pleasant, I led the puppies out of their nursery and put them into a makeshift enclosure at the side of the house. There they had a box that was open in in the front to serve as a sleeping place or as a refuge from the weather. Now they had enough room to practice running, jumping, and wrestling.

Three times a day they were fed a mixture of lean beef or canned meat, puppy chow, milk, and vitamins. They still tried to nurse, but Poco's milk supply was dwindling fast.

When I was present, I let them roam about freely on the lawn, with Poco to help me guard them and to herd them back if they ran off too far. Poco was very patient with them no matter how rough they played with her; but if one pup got out of line and strayed away, she gave a sharp bark and sometimes a nip on the neck and the puppy responded immediately.

The frisky puppies and their mother were fun to watch, and friends and neighbors often stopped by to see them and laugh at their antics. I encouraged people to play with the pups and touch them, since it is very important for puppies between the ages of four and twelve weeks to have contact with humans. This is called socializing. If puppies grow up without any human contact, they will never relate well to people in later life.

At this age a puppy also learns to distinguish between a hard bite and a "soft" bite when it wrestles or play-fights with its littermates or people. This is important, since its tiny, needle-sharp teeth can really hurt. If a puppy between the ages of three and five months has not learned to control its biting, its owner should immediately correct it sternly.

I had not planned to name any of the puppies except for Amber, who had been given his name at birth, because I did not intend to keep them. But everyone asked: Which is this one? or What do you call that one over there? So I gave them temporary identifying names. The second little male was called Timmy, the largest female was Mona, and the small, delicate female was Wendy.

Timmy was gentle and quiet, and he loved people who were quiet and gentle too. He did not like loud noise and rough treatment. To be held and cuddled was his greatest pleasure. But he could also hold his own and defend his rights if the other pups tried to take advantage of him.

Mona was the bold one. She was always eager to explore and try new things and situations. She was very outgoing and friendly with children and grownups alike. She was the first pup to start the fascinating game of untying people's shoelaces, and all the other pups learned it from her. It was almost impossible to break them of this habit.

Amber seemed to be Poco's favorite. She played with him more than with the other puppies. He liked to go off by himself to investigate things—a rock, or a visitor's toes. He was no lap dog and quite unlike Timmy, he protested loudly and struggled hard to free himself if someone picked him up. He was probably the brightest and most mature puppy in the litter.

Wendy was much slower in approaching new situations, and she did not make friends easily. But once she liked and trusted someone, she was devoted and seldom left that person's side. She was still very much a mama's baby and preferred to play or sit with Poco.

At the age of six weeks puppies usually get their first inoculations to protect them against various diseases. Up to this time they were naturally immune from drinking their mother's milk, which carried antibodies.

Now that Poco's pups had stopped nursing completely, this protection would soon be lost. A veterinarian friend who had to attend a sick horse in the neighborhood offered to come over and give the puppies their shots. The little dogs did not mind the needle at all and were interested only in the vet's shoelaces.

I also asked a well-known breeder of Shetland Sheepdogs to come over sometime and tell me what she thought of the puppies. She looked them over carefully and said that she was sure that they were purebred Shelties. We will never know Poco's life story and how she got bred, but I felt more confident that I could find good steady homes for the pups with responsible people. Purebred dogs are not abandoned or passed on to second homes as frequently as mixed-breed dogs are.

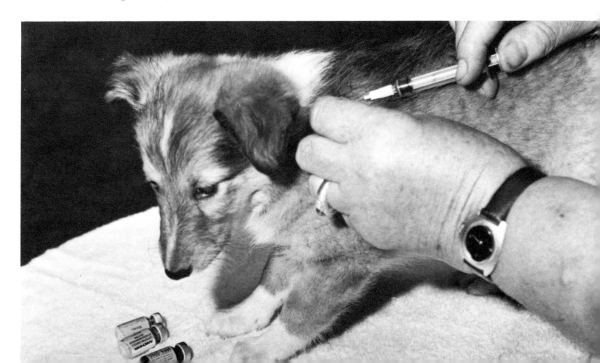

When the puppies were seven weeks old I spread the word around that three Sheltie puppies would be for sale in a few weeks. I had decided to keep Amber for myself. Eight or nine weeks of age is a good time for a puppy to go into a new home. At that age it can manage quite well alone; it is very responsive and trainable and ready to form lasting attachments to human friends.

Several people came to look at the puppies, but I turned them down because their home environment and their temperment were not compatible with the needs of the puppy. I did not want to put quiet Timmy into an active, noisy household or affectionate Wendy in a home where she would be left alone all day long.

One day a family of four came to buy a puppy as a birthday present for the young girl. I liked the way the entire family observed and played with the little dogs before selecting one. The girl held first one puppy, then two, and could not make

up her mind which of the two females she liked best. Then
Mona gave her a wet kiss and the choice was made. I could see
by the happy expression on the girl's face that she and Mona
would be great pals. All this time the girl's brother had played

gently and quietly with Timmy, and an instant bond seemed to have developed between the two. The parents also noticed it and decided that the boy should have a puppy of his own as well. We all agreed it would be nice for the two puppies to grow up together. The young girl carried Mona away in her arms, and the boy led Timmy on a leash. Timmy never glanced back once.

The next day a man came who wanted a puppy as a gift for his wife, who was home alone all day and needed a companion and something to love and care for. Little Wendy was just what he was looking for. He had come prepared with a carrying cage and took Wendy with him.

I put a little red collar on Amber and watched him frolicking with Poco on the lawn. He was loved and spoiled by everyone and showed no signs of missing his sisters or brother.

I felt sure that life was really beginning now for Poco's puppies, since all had found such good homes.

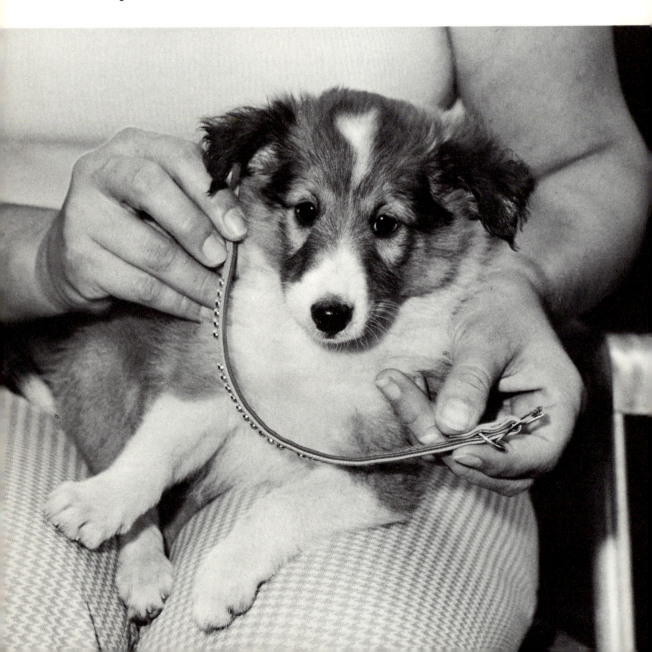